red bean,

wings

Hare Etix

red bean, coke, and wings © 2022 Hare Etix

Presentation by *BookLeaf Publishing*

Web: www.bookleafpub.com

E-mail: info@bookleafpub.com

ISBN: 978-93-95784-41-2

First edition 2022

DEDICATION

to the child i used to be and still aspire to be

living nostalgia

write like a kid again
fuck spelling
        fuck punctuation
i'm reclaiming the childhood i lost
through the words   i quashed

i'll scrawl & scowl & shout & howl
& maybe i'll overuse my exclamation marks!
who says i can't! be! excited!
        be!!
          excited!!!

i want to wake up with my clothes all tidied
ready for my field trip
i want to feel my emotions bubbling like a cauldron
        like the
cauldrons i dreamt
with my potions of toothpaste and soap
        of bubbly little hope

write like a kid again
        with a mind full of creative impulses
        untouched by a world of capitalistic
recluses
& write like the child you're meant to be

please, a favour

can you
carve a place for me in your heart?
not unconditionally,
just temporarily,
i'd like to be loved.

to make tea

there are three easy steps to making tea:

one, a kettle filled with water—
      boiled to the brim—
      steam escaping the hatchet.
      cloaking like a hat's rim,
      snaking around every limb.

two, as the pitch reaches a crescendo
      remove the metal,
      toss in a couple bags, or leaves.
      clean up the stained water memento
      and revel in the soft-pedal treble.

three, add milk, sugar, cream,
      honey for the wealthy.
      let hot mugs burn numb fingers,
      tea cooling when thoughts linger.
      pour the liquid delicacy down a drain—
      not a drop retained
      but fragmented splinters gathered and gained.

funhouse mirror

mirror, clear not glazed,
seems as it states:
run through in carnival funhouse,
keep toxic fumes from consuming,
false high, like nitrous;
endorphins flooding system.
perception altered but infectious "ha ha,"
laugh bounced off reflected smiles.
joy foolish in favoured
jest—
favoured in foolish joy.
smiled reflected off bounced laugh
ha. ha.
infectious altered perception
system flooding
endorphins: nitrous, like high
consuming from fumes, toxic.
keep funhouse carnival,
in—through—run.
states it as seems,
glazed, not clear mirror.

feign shui

a mirror leans in the corner,
between the closet and the door.
it faces the foot of my bed
so if i lean over my head,
i'll see myself instead.

my mom says,
i'll become small, demure,
which feng shui sees, and concurs.
but i like to feign
that it's betwixt cosmos,
maybe a soul will cross plains
and i won't be so lonely tomorrow.

metamorphosis

change & growth.

a dinosaur egg, creaking n' cracking,

evolution, in a way.

dreaming, a cloudy sky turned bright,

and slumber, restful sleep.

intentional silence & purposeful noise.

creating and displacing and discovering and
rediscovering

bold realizations made into reality.

variations in tempo, rhythm, tune,

change is music.

scorched palace

flames are so pretty.

transforming something mundane and grotesque,
into a bright spectacle of fire;
sweltering off the raw sickly resin
dripping down a golden sticky confection.

the pads of my fingers burn to ash
when i cradle radiant embers,
hoping to light myself so luminous.

in a destruction so pure and violent,
the pyre births a life
one oh so brilliant.

and so,
i look upon the devouring bonfire
made of the family brownstone,
and i tell myself,
"flames are so pretty."

fifteen and god forsakes me

driving past a liquor store
at half past four
(i can't drive yet,
but it's freeing to ignore.)

twenty bucks sits by my waist
with an i.d. bare-faced
and before creating chit-chat (what a waste),
i drive past with haste.

but,
with a Sin in motion,
i take five off the gilded devotion.

and, one means two and two means three.
so, gold is pulled down to my palm
as the Devil humbly soothes me.

in dependence

this fourth of july, i read articles of american
tragedies.
i don't live under stars and stripes
but even we hear of columbus sailing the ocean blue.
in a heinous notion,
i wish i were that free too.

trade my meager room for a derelict cabin,
caressing gentle waves on calming nights,
setting sail to a point beyond lights.
maybe there will be nothing
                                nothing beyond a distant
horizon,
i'll sit and stew with the wailing siren.

and truly, i know,
            i know i'll go stir-crazy,
            perhaps get a vicious bout of scurvy.
but the risky unknown still pulls my attention,
calls me away from this noxious surely dependence.

silver-tongued fool

between every scar and wrinkle and mole,
there's a stretch of skin and time
that i tentatively mark as mine.

i see the swirling patterns on cheeks,
i feel the soft ridges peaking knees,
i push the cradling waterfall out of mind,
and i close my eyes and tuck my fists
knowing no one will regard me with
                                    the tenderness i wish.

in the end,
i'm a silver-tongued fool,
worshipping the deities who roam the land
with a wholly unflourished peony in hand.

believe me

what's the kidney?
i don't know but it aches something terrible—
it rips along my guts,
putting skin to teeth, flesh from bone.

my eyes drip something hazy
and i want someone to believe me
                someone to hear me, see me, need me.
need someone to pull my chin up,
bring a chillingly temperate hand to my pounding
temple,
someone to consider the pale sweating, torso shaking,
face crumpling.

lay me to rest with a palm of liquid gold.
kiss the injury of my gut,
as a loving mother would a cut.
resolve the ache in decade-old bones for a day,
a day with a heart too cold.

defiant

it's a fine establishment.

they clamp hooks into my soft palate,
dragging out sinful confessions
of loving habits.

i'm a defiant child,
they'll say as i stare down the diplomat
who takes my childish passion
as merciless permission.

no matter how long i doubt,
they continue to pry
from my bullet-torn mouth.

(but, they're right,
i'm defiant
and i'll spitefully shout it
inwards and out)

stubborn little kid

there's a little kid pounding in my chest,
gnawing on my sternum,
pulling my ribs from my tergum.

nails torn: red, raw, gone.
on and on,
reaching into the deepest morceau
of my desperate torso.

i can only look on in awe
at the stubborn drive
lost to nails torn raw.

absent-minded

a little absent-minded.
brain looping a clouded visage,
draping down a muddied façade.

no one glimpses beyond the vision we uphold,
blanking as shutters unfold,
over the windows into my soul.

i'm a little absent-minded.
lost to the dreams of abstract love,
dreams of fame and fortune—
ridding penniless portions.

swallowing distant mumbled phrase,
to return a troubled craze
in a gloomy wonderless world.

still, a little absent-minded.

prickly/sensitive

māmā calls me mǐngǎn (敏感),
sensitive.
tears dribble valleys into my cheeks,
sensitive.
strong boys don't cry,
they look into the sun with squinted eyes,
and they certainly are not
sensitive.

roses are delicate, māmā says
when i pluck one from the garden.
but māmā adores them,
even if delicate is synonymous with sensitive.

if i can't be sensitive like me,
maybe i'll be delicate like a rosy sea.

then, māmā calls me zháshǒu (扎手),
prickly like a rose.
difficult to handle.
argumentative.
but at least, i'm no longer
sensitive.

pamplemousse

first grade spelling test, ever the over-achiever,
scribbled lines out on porcelain tiles,
hair-lined trigger of fiery coils.
letter after letter eroding a fragile sentience,
just last week, i came into existence.
it's a fruitless labour of ambition
~~(ironic, scratch in pomme again)~~

how to remember words of such contradiction
~~(ananas, a pineapple not banana)~~

molding thoughts to sound like limericked evolutions
~~(une poire, fraise, orange, pêche)~~
~~(pompl)~~
grains of fading sanity disperse
~~(pomplle)~~
can accept less than the worst
~~(pamplmu)~~
only so much to rehearse
~~(pamplim)~~
limited satisfaction when it works
~~(pome)~~
put so much stock in a simple verse
~~(pomle)~~
the hold it has so perverse
~~(pmpele)~~
lie in my bed, a choking hearse
pamplemousse.

god's spitting image

it's a miracle of creation, a bean to swallow
maybe a swan or a dove or a crane to follow?
declare it to a hoard
or keep it discreet
truly, it's impertinent and obsolete

one of three hundred
                              eighty-five
                                              thousand
that day
a mumbling void came screeching to play

a yank, a mark
a cry, life's spark
sprouting out "god's image,"
from adam—from eve; up & leave
noah's ark

with flailing limbs and vital force
maybe—i'll live and let live,
a life on it's course.

personhood

hm.

Ingram Content Group UK Ltd.
Milton Keynes UK
UKHW020816060623
422954UK00016B/989